Riad Sattouf

ESTHER'S NOTEBOOKS

Tales from my 10-year-old life

Translated from the French by Sam Taylor

PUSHKIN PRESS

The Family

My name is Esther and I'm 9 years old. I live in Paris, in the 17th arrondissement.

My dad is a sports trainer or something in this place where people go to do sport. My mum works in a bank.

They've been together a long time. There's a photo of them when they were young on the fridge.

I have a big brother called Antoine. We share the same bedroom. He gave me some headphones so I wouldn't bother him. He doesn't like any of my music.

I'm in Year 5 at a private school. My dad says it's better for me at my age.

My brother goes to a normal school that my parents don't pay for. In the morning he feels sick and doesn't want to go. He's not a very good student.

My best friend at school is Eugenie. I like Cassandra too. Actually I get on pretty well with everybody.

At school, we can talk to each other how we want. It's not like being at home, where you're not allowed to swear.

But I don't like to swear much. It's trashy, not classy. Boys are trashy, for example. They swear all the time when they're doing two things: playing football and talking to girls. But anyway, who cares about boys?

Eugenie is really lucky because she's rich. She already has the iPhone 6! And at home she's got an iPad and a computer and she even has a TV in her bedroom.

If I could just have an iPhone – even a 4 – I'd be so happy. But I'm poor.

I'm even the poorest one in my family.

(Based on a true story told by Esther, who is 9 years old)

Riad Sattouf

Mums and Dads

Panel 1: I've been going to this school since I was 6. Most of the other students are the same.

This is me drinking a carton of apple juice that my mum gave me

My best friend Eugenie

Cassandra

It's break time

Panel 2: We play quite a few games. My favourite is Mums and Dads.

Hey, shall we go shopping?

Cooool, it's Mums and Dads!

That's how the game starts

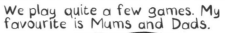

Violet   Olympia   Lea

Panel 3: Eugenie is always the mum. Cassandra is the baby. I'm the teenager. And it's the same in the other family — they always play the same roles.

Naughty baby, you threw up EVERY-WHERE!

My baby's got a fever!

Panel 4: Hey, what can we do?

You teenagers need to leave us in peace so we can look after the babies. Here's lots of money, now go shopping!

WHOAH!

COOOOL

Can't you see we're busy?

Panel 5: I don't know where the dads are in this game. They're never around. They're working.

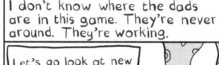

Let's go look at new dresses.

Good idea

Panel 6: The shopping centre is near the trees.

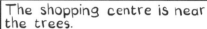

This outfit is gooorrr-geous!

Mmm, it really is!

And look at that one!

Panel 7: When we've bought our clothes, we put them on and parade in front of the mums and babies.

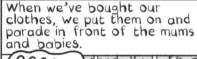

OOOOOH

Sweet, yo!

Violet strikes poses

Panel 8:

Panel 9: BYOO-TI-FULL

Me, looking hot

Panel 10: The mums and babies vote for the hottest model. The winner gets a Nintendo DS and an iPhone!

I always win!

YEEAAH!

PFFT

If Violet's really sad at losing, I give her the DS

We pretend we're holding them in our hands!

Panel 11: Sometimes, Violet and I find the others playing Mums and Dads without us!

?   ?

My baby was good

So was mine

Panel 12: Hey, why are you playing without us?

Panel 13: We're not playing. We're pregnant.

Sorry

Panel 14:

Mwah

We leave them in peace.

(Based on a true story told by Esther, who is 9 years old)

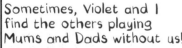

Antoine

My brother Antoine and I sleep in the same room. He's 14 and he's a bit stupid, but that's normal for a boy.

This is me reading "Stars Like", a very interesting magazine about stars

YO, HOMIE♫

At ten o'clock, my dad comes to switch off the light. But Antoine keeps listening to his trashy music in bed.

The singer's name is La Fouine (that means "The Weasel")

Get your gun and shoot him in the head WE DON'T GIVE A FUCK! Can't buy it in stores we sell in bulk instead WE DON'T GIVE A FUCK!

He whispers the lyrics

I'm in my Porsche, eating a kebab WE DON'T GIVE A FUCK! Talk shit about me, better watch yo' back COS WE DON'T GIVE A FUCK!

He looks really annoyed

So I stick my fingers in my ears and imagine someone's given me a KidiSecrets.

It's an electronic diary for keeping your secrets safe!

The screen is heart-shaped — cool.

FOR ME? ☆

My dad hates them

Esther! Pssst! Esther! Hey!

Can you tell me about your day, with loads of details? That way, I might be able to fall asleep...

HUH? OH PFFT!

I'LL DO THE SAME FOR YOU!

Pleeeaaase

PFFT... All right then, I got up and I went to the kitchen for

NO, more details! How many steps did you take? Tell me everything.

Okay, let's see... One step to put my first foot out of bed, and another to stand up... After that, one step to put on my left slipper, no, I mean my right, but... well, sometimes it's the left...

That's it...

And then, one step, two steps, hang on... one, two, three... four steps to the door...

Mmm

He always falls asleep before I drink my hot chocolate.

ZZZZZ

Psst! Antoine! Are you asleep? It's your turn to tell me about your day!

AN-TOINE!

... I got up and I went to my shitty school and then I went to bed and that's it...

ZZZZZ

(Based on a true story told by Esther, who is 9 years old)

Riad Sattouf

Kidnapper Alert

Panel 1: I have a great social life. My friends really love me.

This is me in the playground, listening to my friend Eugenie who's telling me about a photograph

It's break time

?!?

... and my cousin's laughing and he shows me his phone and I see a photo of TAL with a boy "doing things" on the beach! I WAS SHOCKED, YO!

Panel 2: I don't know what to say about boys except that we don't talk about them because they're, you know, boys.

What things?

Y'know, kissing and stuff

The boys are playing over there

The girls are here

Panel 3: Boys are nasty. They're supposed to be nasty. It's normal, that's just how they are. But sometimes they go too far.

ZLATAN! ZLATAN!

YEAH FUCKING ZLATAN

They shout that when they score a goal

Panel 4: For example, the other day, me, Eugenie, Cassandra and Violet were playing something, I can't remember what...

Oh, you're so beautiful

Hee hee

My name is Rapunzel, what's yours?

Panel 5: ... when suddenly boys started running from all directions to kidnap us.

They were being quiet and looked really mean

Panel 6: A kidnapping is when lots of boys get together and decide to take a girl to one of their friends. They force her and it's bad but it doesn't happen very often.

KIDNAPPER ALERT

KIDNAPPER ALERT!

Panel 7: At first, I thought they were going to kidnap me (I've been kidnapped loads before and that day I was wearing my red dress and velvet boots) but actually they came for Violet.

Mpf! Mpf!

Panel 8: They took her to the boy who'd ordered the kidnapping (it was Maxime, a big show-off who all the girls hate) and she started crying. She knew she would never see her parents again.

You're mine till you die.

WAAAAH

Panel 9: Us girls tried to save her but the other boys hit us. So we went to fetch the teacher, Miss Morret (the ugly one).

Miss! Violet's been kidnapped!

It's bad, yo!

?

She's always looking at her phone even though we're not allowed to

Panel 10: The teacher went over and yelled at the boys. Maxime managed not to cry.

WHAT'S THE BIG DEAL?

Panel 11: Violet started shouting too then and she told the teacher to leave Maxime alone because she belonged to him now.

GET YOUR HANDS OFF MY HUSBAND!

Panel 12: In the end, everybody cried. So that's what boys are like. Bad.

And I really thought Violet was too ugly to ever be kidnapped!

WAAAH

WAAAAH

(Based on a true story told by Esther, who is 9 years old)

6

The Popular Singer

Panel 1: Me and my brother don't talk much, but we watch TV together.

On Saturday, we were alone in the house because our parents were out shopping

Panel 2: My brother had the remote and we were watching NRJ HIT MUSIC ONLY, a really cool TV channel that shows music videos.

Helloooo yoohoo!

Yesss this song rocks

Panel 3: This track is dedicated to Mrs Pavoshko! You remember? Mr Diallo!

You know this one, right?

Yeah!

Panel 4: The singer is called Black M and I think he's one of the most popular singers in France. But it's mostly boys who like him.

Hey, Mrs Pavoshko, yo
I'm not in prison or a mental hospital, no
I'm a star, Mrs Pavoshko
And your kids dig me, Mrs Pavoshko

Panel 5: In this song, he's talking about a school headmistress who didn't believe in him, so he takes his revenge in the song.

Yo, you remember me, the little black kid who wrote crazy verses like Fuck the Teacher? Pass me the mic!

FUCK THE TEACHER

I was hoping I could watch "Tangled" again

Panel 6: I like that song, it's catchy and Black M is very handsome (that's also why he's very popular).

I don't give a BEEP yeah
Yeah, I know, it's a shame
I'm being censored
and you're to blame
YEAH YEAH YEAH!

Panel 7: My brother knew all the words to the song. He's good at learning, so I don't know why he's so bad at school.

All alone, head under-water, I thought it's time to start a fire!

START A FIRE!

Panel 8: But my parents came home and my dad recognized the song straight away.

TURN THAT RUBBISH OFF NOW!

HUH? YOU SERIOUS, YO?

All alone, head under water, I thought...

Panel 9: THAT TUNE IS A DISEASE! YOU CATCH IT WITHOUT EVEN NOTICING AND IT STAYS IN YOUR HEAD FOR DAYS! TURN IT OFF NOW, I DON'T WANT TO HEAR IT!

I'M LISTENING TO THIS!

It's time to start a fire...

Panel 10: My dad teaches sport so he's much stronger than Antoine. So he changed the channel.

Come on, an advertising jingle, anything...

And this is REALLY good news...

Panel 11: Mrs Pavoshko was right when she said that guy would be a waste of space! That song is rubbish!

How can anyone like that crap?

Yeah, like you've got really good taste in music!

Panel 12: Dad put on a programme he likes on RMC Discovery. It's about men driving very fast cars. But it was too late: the tune was stuck in his head.

All alone, head underwater, I thought it's time to start a fire
GRRRRR!

I didn't dare ask if I could watch "Tangled"

Oh my word, that's five seconds faster than Harry

(Based on a true story told by Esther, who is 9 years old)

Riad Sattouf

7

Maxime

A private school is a school you have to pay for. I don't really know why my dad chose this school, because we're not rich.

I'll explain why later. It's better for girls your age. You don't get so many thugs in private schools.

My dad is very stylish

I love him

I think he's scared that the boys will hurt me. He's right — boys are horrible. In my class, for example, Maxime is super-nasty.

Hello bitch!

Sometimes he would spit at us for no reason.

WHAT'S WRONG WITH YOU?

YO, IT'S ALL OVER YOU

Actually he mostly spat at Cassandra

Ha ha

He did impressions of us in class in front of everyone. The girls really hated him.

Miiisss, can I go to the toilets?

Miiisss, can I go poo-poo?

HA HA

HA HAHA

HA HA

And then, the other day, he got out of his dad's car and he wasn't dressed the same way any more.

CLACK!

His dad is very very rich

He came into the playground and started swaggering around like a <u>cool dude</u>, listening to music on headphones.

Everybody fell silent. All the girls stared at him.

Huh, what's he doing?

He's got Blueteeth headphones, did you see?

But that's against the...

I went to talk to Maxime because nobody else dared.

HEY! YOU'RE NOT ALLOWED TO WEAR HEADPHONES IN THE PLAYGROUND, I'M GOING TO TELL THE TEACHER!

HAHA SHUT UP... YOU THINK I'M SCARED?

I'VE GOT THE SAME JACKET AS MAITRE GIMS, BITCH.

Maitre Gims is the most famous person in France. He's a singer that everybody likes. He's the most popular boy ever.

You never see his eyes

This is him at the start of the video for "Changer", a really cool song

He's very rich: he shows off his tablet in the video

Lenco

I didn't even need to tell the teacher. She confiscated his headphones and his baseball cap.

Seriously, yo, it's too much, showing off like that!

Cassandra, what's the matter?

Waaah!

He... sniff... he's too good-looking... like a star... and... and... he hates me!

Waaah!

Maxime always spat at Cassandra. But, just like all the other girls at school, she'd fallen in love with him.

(Based on a true story told by Esther, who is 9 years old)

Mitchell

My dad says boys in private schools aren't as crazy as ones in schools you don't have to pay for (yes, my dad thinks boys are crazy, and he's right).

This is me in my favourite dress blowing in the wind

The worst boy in my class, the one all the girls really hate, is Mitchell.

Don't you want to play with me?

SHUT YOUR MOUTH

I don't like swear words but I say them to him

He wants to play with girls!!!

The other boys hate him because they're nasty, but we hate him because he doesn't understand anything about life.

Just one time! At the game you like!

GO AWAY! STOP FOLLOWING US!!!

WE TOLD YOU: NEVER!

He's English or something

He's really poor, for a start. He doesn't like gadgets, he doesn't have a phone, and he kisses his dad in front of everybody.

Have a good day, my boy

Speaking English

MWAH

Plus he's extremely ugly and his body is weird. He runs with his back straight, like a robot.

Eugenie's really good at copying him

HU! HU! HU!

EVERYBODY GET IN LINE

This is us in PE

But the worst thing is that he keeps on being nice even though everybody hates him.

PASS THE FUCKING BALL!

FUCK

Even the boys pretend he doesn't exist

But he still runs around with them like everything is normal

The other day, he did something terrible.

VIOLET, I... I LOVE YOU...

?

GASP

HUH

HUH

Violet was shocked, so she and her friends grabbed Mitchell and beat him up.

They hurt him really badly. And then the teacher saw them.

Waaah!

Violet and her friends were punished, and Mitchell went to a corner and cried and cried.

WAAAAH!

WAAAH!

Anyway, despite that, the other day, he did something else really bad. It was the end of term, so the teacher gave us all Kinder eggs.

KINDER EGGS, MY FAVOURITE THING IN THE WHOLE WORLD!

Who hasn't had their

Okay then, you can have mine, Esther!

I hesitated, but it was a Kinder, the best thing in the world, so I took it.

Thanks

GASP

OMG

WHAAT

HUH

HAHAHA!

SHHH, THAT'S ENOUGH

SHE LOVES HIM

HAHA

HA

HAHA

Esther loves Mitchell

Mitchell really is the worst boy in the world.

(Based on a true story told by Esther, who is 9 years old)

Riad Sattouf

Bendy Bodies

I want to be a singer when I'm older. A famous singer, like TAL, for example (she's got dark hair and the voice of an angel).

I've noticed something. Popular, famous people are very good-looking, but they also have something else in common: bendy bodies.

Tal, for example, she's a really good mover. Dynamic.

Yannick Noah is very good-looking (and very famous), and I heard he used to be a sports teacher, like Dad.

My dad is very very good-looking. And he can do the splits too.

Papa can also stand on his hands and bend over backwards.

The president of France... what's his name again? Oh yes, Hollande. Anyway, he's good-looking, of course, because you can't be president if you're ugly. But I don't know how bendy he is (I suppose he must be).

It's normal that celebrities are good-looking. People are inspired when they see people who are better-looking than them.

For example, our teacher Miss Morret is really really ugly. Nobody's inspired by her.

Or the woman who lives in the office near the front door of our apartment building.

Or my mum, for example... She was very beautiful when she was young. Nowadays, she's not as bendy as she used to be.

Not that she really tries very hard.

Thankfully, I take more after my dad.

(Based on a true story told by Esther, who is 9 years old)

10

Gays

My school is a primary school, for kids aged 6 to 11.

This is me arriving in the playground with some of the younger kids (I don't talk to them)

A funny thing happened this week. A boy from Year 2 walked past carrying his schoolbag and it touched Abdou's bottom.

Abdou is a big boy from Year 6 who's tall enough to be in secondary school. His dad works in politics or something.

OI! DON'T TOUCH MY ARSE, YOU QUEER!

?

QUEER!

? ! ? ??

Hey Abdou, what's "QUEER"?

Gays, you know? They're gross...

Really nice gay

!

I know what gays are: two men who love each other (two bald men, usually). Sometimes they can be women, but that's rare.

URGH ESTHER YOU'RE QUEER, YO

HA HA

After that, everybody in the playground started calling each other queer. It was really funny.

HAHA gotcha Esther!

DON'T TOUCH ME, YOU QUEER!

You're a QUEER

She's QUEER

HA

The next day, that little Year 2 kid pointed at Abdou, who was wearing a blue watch and an orange jacket.

Blue and orange are the colours of queers!

?

WAK!

Afterwards, Abdou was so angry that he told a monitor about the Year 2 kid.

And then he said I was queer, sir, he can't say that

I'm not queer, sir

Why did he say that?

He never notices anything

I don't think there are any gays in my school. Oh, wait, I did see two Year 6 boys kissing and rolling on the ground in front of everybody.

I was shocked

I don't see the point in being gay. You can't have children. Violet told me that she and her parents had gone on a protest march to stop gays adopting.

We chanted "A mum and a dad, every child deserves that"!

It was great!

It must be horrible having two dads! Can you imagine? They'd never be home because they were too busy working, and they wouldn't be able to cook or keep the house clean...

Aren't you hungry?

I'm really hungry

You go! You go!

HA HA

But when you think about it, it's weird that people think being gay is a bad thing. I don't really know what that's about.

And Mum's not even home yet...

And it takes her so long to get dinner ready...

Yeah HAHA

(Based on a true story told by Esther, who is 9 years old)

Riad Sattouf

11

The Mystery of Father Christmas

I really like going in shops, especially when it's Christmas (I like the decorations).

This is my family at a giant shopping centre called Velizy 2

Before I stopped believing in Father Christmas, I saw so many strange things.

For a start, when we went to Auchan, just before Christmas, there were always more toys than usual. And the people around us all had trolleys full of toys.

Why are they buying them when Father Christmas will bring them for free?

The weird thing is that my dad told me magic and God didn't exist, but Father Christmas did.

Hey Antoine, Father Christmas doesn't exist, does he?

Well I don't give a...

Antoine

Answer your little sister. Go on, sweetheart!

Um, oh... Well, yeah, he does exist... um...

Nooo! Seriously, you still believe? At your age?

My dad told me that God, Jesus and magic were all invented by intelligent people to manipulate less intelligent people without them realizing.

Hey, you shouldn't threaten your son like that, wallah

"Wallah"? That's new!

But it's obvious that God and Jesus don't exist: you only ever see paintings of them, never photographs.

Ha ha what rubbish!

Shhh, sweet-heart.

This is us visiting a church in La Rochelle last summer

Mathilde, in my class, told me she met Jesus in a church once.

He smiled at me. I sat on his lap and touched his beard!

Hee hee

REALLY?

When I visited the church in La Rochelle, I also saw someone who looked like Jesus, but it was just a homeless man.

Anyway, after a while, my dad finally admitted that everybody gave each other presents at Christmas, and it had nothing to do with Father Christmas.

I knew it!

So last year, I knew who'd given me each present (Mum and Dad: the flying fairy, Granny: nature cards)... until I found an incredible present that I hadn't asked for but I'd really wanted!

My granny

THE GLACIATION PLASMA POKEMON! WHO GAVE ME THIS?

Huh?   Was it you?

Um, not me   No

GASP!

Incredible but true: nobody had given me that present! But there it was! Since then, I've started believing in Father Christmas again.

(Based on a true story told by Esther, who is 9 years old)

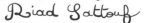
Riad Sattouf

12

The Truth About Father Christmas

This year, we went to my granny's house for Christmas, like we do almost every year.

This is me in a street in Bain-de-Bretagne, the place where she lives

She lives in a small house, and in the house next door I have a friend I see every year because she visits her grandparents at Christmas too.

Eugenie!!!

Hi there!

Her name is Eugenie too, like my friend in Paris! Weird, huh?

We're allowed to go on the path behind our houses. So on the day before Christmas, we went for a walk.

Listen to this, it's the NRJ MUSIC AWARDS 2014 compilation... "Andalouse" by Kendji Girac... I got it for Christmas...

WHAT? BUT CHRISTMAS IS TOMORROW! HOW DID...

Yeah, but we gave each other presents yesterday because my dad has to go back to work today...

Ebony eyes, I like to see you move like a queen, your body glides...

Kendji Girac is a famous singer and a gypsy (I don't know what that means)

And there it was: the proof that Father Christmas didn't actually exist.

I was about to start crying when suddenly...

GASP!

BRR!

It came towards us. It was so SO beautiful! It looked at us.

BRHH

It smelled of horse

You could see its muscles!

! !

In a flash, I no longer cared that Father Christmas didn't exist! I was crazy about that horse.

My friend ran away

AGHH

But she loved it too

Afterwards, me and Eugenie went to her house and started a horse-lovers' club that we called "Horse Stars". It's for sharing information between people who are interested in horses.

We googled all the possible horse colours and wrote them down on a sheet of paper, in case anyone was interested

– Cremello
– perlino
– palomino...

And then, on Christmas Eve...

So what do you think Father Christmas's secret present will be this year, sweetheart?

Granny

Dad

My brother Antoine

Mum

BLAH BLAH BLAH I KNOW THE TRUTH SO STOP TELLING ME RUBBISH. I KNOW FATHER CHRISTMAS DOESN'T EXIST.

But I would like you to buy me a horse next Christmas.

Everybody was shocked, but at least things were clear now.

What the...

Just to be clear, before everybody blames me, I didn't tell her.

(Based on a true story told by Esther, who is 9 years old)

Riad Sattouf

13

The Charlie

(Based on a true story told by Esther, who is 9 years old)

The Wedding

This week, something amazing happened: I finally got married.

This is me in the playground, listening to Eugenie tell me about "Strictly Come Dancing"

... because Alizee is SO jealous of Nathalie Pechalat and...

It would take too long to explain

I'd never told anyone about it, but I was secretly in love with a boy (in fact, I was secretly in love with three boys, but let's forget about the other two).

This is the boy I love

I'll play up front

Louis, my husband, is best friends with Maxime, the richest and most popular boy in school (the one who has the same jacket as Maitre Gims).

We used to look at each other from a distance

Maxime

His gorgeous smile

Then, the other morning, he got someone to give me this note.

The truth is the opposite LOL

Esther,
I don't like you and your stupid L (you know who)
P.S. what about you?

It was the most beautiful note I'd ever read in my life.

So we agreed to meet up in a corner of the playground and...

We kissed!!!!

MWAH

?

Whassup, yo?

Five minutes later, everybody was staring at us.

I saw them kissing. With tongues!

Gasp

Whoa

Huh

Eugenie yelled "They kissed! Now they have to get married! Wed-ding! Wed-ding!"

WED-DING!

Everybody was yelling it, even the Year 6 kids

WED-DING! WED-DING! DO IT NOW!

Yes, it was the most amazing day of my life

WED-DING!

So we got married. The whole school watched us. It was CRAZY.

Eugenie brought the Rainbow Loom wedding rings

I now pronounce you man and wife!

Violet was the priest

HA HA

YOU MAY NOW SNOG THE BRIDE!

AND YOU'LL BE TOGETHER FOR ETERNITY!

Hee Hee

And we did it in front of everybody.

The next day, I realized that everybody in school knew who I was.

They all stared at me in awe, even the Year 6 kids

And the Year 2 kids too

Even the monitor, who's normally really mean, well now he was being nice.

Sooo... How's married life?

I'm married!

But the best thing was when Maxime asked one of his friends to give me a note.

It's crazy because Louis is supposed to be his friend!

i know your thinking bout me you love me i know cuz i c*** you too guess what
MAX

I think I'm now the most popular girl in the school. Crazy, isn't it?

Yo, how you doing babe?

Hee hee

But that doesn't matter anymore because Louis and me are man and wife for eternity.

(Based on a true story told by Esther, who is 9 years old)

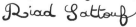

15

Turning 10

This week, I turned 10 years old.

This is me and my family celebrating my birthday at Pizza Pino because their Four-Cheese pizza is my favourite meal in the whole world

I got a flower-patterned jacket as a present.

Exactly what I wanted

BYOO-TI-FUL

The next day, I put it on and went to school.

Yo, what's good is that it's your own style, I mean it wouldn't suit me, for example...

My friend Eugenie

I went to see Louis, my husband (we got married last week, remember). He was with his friends.

Hello, lover.

Whoa, pink flowers, fuck me!

?

He didn't come to my birthday party.

Louis will be here soon, he

You think? I got a text from Violet saying he's been with Elodie all day...

Oh yeah I knew that course I did um

This is me trying hard not to cry

In fact, he got a divorce without telling me. Now he has another wife.

AN PRIX

WE BUY SILVER AND GOLD

CASH IN HAND

Please don't tell my mum what I did with it

One of the zombies took the coat and good luck to them (I call them "zombies" because they walk slowly and hold out their hands and moan. They're not really zombies because they're not dead, just very poor. I'm really scared that I'll end up like them).

(Based on a true story told by Esther, who is 10 years old)

Riad Sattouf

The Curse

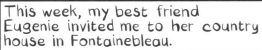

(Based on a true story told by Esther, who is 10 years old)

The Fly

 It's really annoying having to share my bedroom. But we have no choice because we're not very rich.

This is me listening to Voltage FM

My brother Antoine is so horrible, he enjoys watching others suffer (but it's normal because he's a boy).

This is him. I hate him

 Estheeer!

 Bzzzz A FLYYYYYYY

I know this is weird, but the things that scare me most in the world are flies.

 Honestly, this drawing terrifies me

I can't even look at it

Even just talking about them, I feel like I'm about to cry.

 THE FLY IS HEEERE

People say they're not, but I feel sure that flies are intelligent.

 Hey, it's landed on you!

Boys are disgusting

They fly right at me and I'm sure they're trying to get in my nostrils or my ears or my mouth.

 AARRGGHH Bzzzz

 THE FLY! THE FLY IS HERE! QUE PASA? *My dad, the hero* AARRGGHH

 THE FLY! THE FLY SHUT IT!

My dad is an angel.

I've never met anyone like him.

 CLAK

 I find it really hard to believe he's a boy.

(Based on a true story told by Esther, who is 10 years old)

Riad Sattouf

The Popular Boys

Panel 1: I've always gone to this private school. I've never been anywhere else.

This is me walking into the playground

In my school, you're not allowed to wear a baseball cap or have footballer hair

Panel 2: My dad says that in free schools, the boys are violent to girls, and they're crazy.

ESTHER I'M GOING TO KIIIIIILLL YOU

HHH

AGH!

My brother

Panel 3: I think he's right, because my brother Antoine is in a free school and he's a total nutcase.

HA HA HA

NAH I'M NOT REALLY GOING TO KILL YOU, SIS

HA HA

Panel 4: The other day, he came home from school and he kept asking my mum if we were originally from another country.

Nope, we're just from Paris

Even if you go back a long way? Y'know, grannies and all that

No, sorry

Panel 5: So there aren't any Rebeus in our family?

Or any Renois?

No? Hmm...

Panel 6:

Panel 7: MUUUUUUUUM?

WHAT ARE REBEUS AND RENOIS?

Panel 8: So he explained to us that Rebeus were Arabs and Renois were blacks, and how all the popular boys in his school have foreign origins...

Stefan, representing Romania

Always in my heart

I'm Enzo the Italiano, whassup yo

Amar, Senegal 1 France 0 for life yo

Hey, this is Amine the Tunisiano.

Reprezent!

They all have footballer hair

Panel 9: The others are just boring "Babtous" (which means whites).

My name is Gaspard, I'm from Paris

I'm Thomas

...

No footballer hair because Dad said no

Panel 10: So all the Babtous tried to find foreign origins, however distant.

Yo, I'm Gaspard and I represent Portugal...

Don't try anything

Toto from España!

...

(His uncle's wife is Portuguese)

(Half-Spanish great-grandfather)

Panel 11: My dad never agrees with Antoine, so he started yelling at him.

Who cares about origins? That's nationalism, being proud of your origins! All the world's problems are caused by nationalism!

Rise above it!

Panel 12: Come on, Dad, please, just let me get a Jeremy Menez haircut! Pleeease!

NO

Jeremy Menez, A.C. Milan

Panel 13: Hey, wait, Granny's from Brittany! You just have to call yourself "Antoine the Bretonno"

Smart girl!

Well yeah!

(Based on a true story told by Esther, who is 10 years old)

Riad Sattouf

The Baby Cat

Some of my friends went skiing in the February holidays. We went to my grandmother's house in Bain-de-Bretagne.

My dad My mum My brother My granny The rain HA HA And me

In my opinion, God probably doesn't exist, because he never granted the two wishes I made to him.

Oh Lord let me be blonde and please let me have an iPhone

Your humble servant, Esther

For the 14,259th time, no iPhone before secondary school.

Go play with Eugenie.

Boooring

Pardon?

When I go to my grandmother's house, I play with my friend Eugenie (the other Eugenie, I mean, not the one from Paris). I see her every time I come here because she visits her granny during the holidays too.

Look, it's a game where you look after a cat

WHOA TOO COOL

She has an iPad all to herself

It's only the best game in the whole wide world! It's called "My Angela" or something like that.

If you stroke it, the baby cat purrs

prrrrrr prrrr

The bathroom is pink – beautiful

The idea is that you have to look after the baby cat and it's just like a real baby: in the game, it grows up and turns into a teenage cat and then a woman cat.

CLAK CLAK

You can even hit it and then it falls over, it's super-realistic

Ah Ah

You have to feed it, brush its teeth, give it baths and put it to bed, and like that you win gold coins.

Mmm! Glub glub!

CLING CLING

And then, with the gold coins, you can buy dresses or hairstyles, but they're really expensive.

A few examples:

Afro hair (1,680 coins)

Long blonde hair (25 diamonds)

Hipster hat (1,080 coins)

Tiara (75 diamonds)

Hair shaved on one side (free)

Floppy hat (3,000 coins)

And if you want more, you have to buy diamonds.

I'm going to buy 4,000, that's 99 euros... That way, we can buy everything. I know my dad's password – it's my name.

4,000 diamonds = 440,000 coins

Since we were very rich, we bought everything, even the food. But the cat didn't want to eat so Eugenie hit it – it was horrible.

EAT, DAMN YOU! COME ON, EAT!

CLAK CLAK CLAK CLAK CLAK CLAK

It made me cry

She was crazy

After a few days, Eugenie's dad came into our room and he slapped his daughter.

They'd emailed him the 99 euros receipt

CLAK

He took away her iPad for ever.

You can go home, Esther. Eugenie is grounded for the rest of the holiday.

Waaaah

MIAOWW mummy I'm hungry... mummy where are you?

(Based on a true story told by Esther, who is 10 years old)

Racism

Panel 1: My dad says there's lots of violence in free schools. That's why he sends me to a private school. He's worried about me (I love him).

This is me

Thankfully he doesn't know that there are fights in my school too

NG!

Panel 2: I know exactly what racism is. It's fear of people with colours.

It's not just that. It's also thinking that there are different races of human beings...

And that some are superior to others...

Yeah, my race is superior to Esther's, yo

My dad who I love

Panel 3: Being racist is the worst thing in the world.

If you ever become racist, I'll disown you!

Hee hee

My brother who's such an idiot that nobody cares what he says

Panel 4: In my school, it's mostly whites. But there is a Chinese boy, for example (well I don't know if he's Chinese but he does have slanty eyes). He's in Year 3 and NOBODY ever talks to him.

Come on Esther, we're going to play tag

He stays near the pillar at break time and just waits for it to end

I think I heard the teacher calling him 'Jean-Luc' once, which seems a weird name for a Chinese boy

Panel 5: And there are also two brothers, one of them in Year 4 and the other in Year 5. They're always together when they play football and I think they're Arabs.

They're typical boys – just as stupid as the others

Fuck!

Fucking pass it!

Panel 6: Nobody is racist to them at school. Or not that I've ever seen.

GOAAAAAAAAAAL

BENZEMA, WHAT A SHOT!

They're really good at football

Panel 7: And then there's my second-best friend, Cassandra – she's black. It's weird though, it's like she's racist against herself. It makes me sad.

I'm soooo ugly...

Shh, you know that's not true...

Yes it is, I'm blaaack, it suuucks

We have hugs at break time

Panel 8: She has family problems: she doesn't know her father and her mother is all alone. I don't even know what I'd do if I didn't have my dad. I think I'd die.

My mum said that after I was born, my dad went back to Martinique because it was too cold for him in Paris.

I've never seen him since then.

Panel 9: Sometimes I wonder if he thinks about me. When it's sunny in Paris, I think maybe he'd like it here...

Then she cries a bit, and afterwards we talk about something else

Panel 10: I don't see why anybody cares about the colour of someone's skin. What matters in life is being beautiful.

I'm okay – I'm quite pretty

Panel 11: And to be beautiful, you have to be blonde and bendy.

Me at dance class

Legs moving side to side smack it in the air

When I'm 18, I'll dye my hair

Panel 12: It doesn't matter if you're Chinese, Arab, white, black or even fat, if you're blonde and bendy, you'll succeed.

Wave your hands side to side put it in the air

Panel 13: Best example: Beyoncé.

Blonde

+ black

+ very fat

+ super-bendy

+ super-rich

= perfect

(Based on a true story told by Esther, who is 10 years old)

Riad Sattouf

21

Eugenie

I like our apartment, even if I'd prefer to have a room of my own.

This is me with my family watching "It's Only TV"

They're funny

HAHA

HAHA BRILLIANT!

Okay, now for the yoghurt challenge

On Saturday, I went to my friend Eugenie's apartment. It's the biggest apartment I've ever seen. I think her parents are billionaires.

I need the toilet

Fifth door on the right!

They have houses everywhere. But it's funny, their places are always a mess.

Even in the bathroom!

When I came out of the bathroom, this is what I said to Eugenie.

Every time I come to your place, I think "How can they live in such a pigsty?"

Oh yeah? Well, every time I go to your place, I think "How can they live in a place smaller than our toilet?"

THAT IS THE WORST AND MOST HORRIBLE THING ANYONE HAS EVER SAID TO ME.

(Based on a true story told by Esther, who is 10 years old)

Riad Sattouf

22

Zits

Panel 1: My dad is very protective of me (which is normal, because he's my dad).

This is us in the bathroom →

Panel 2: He's afraid that I'll be harassed by boys. He's always asking me if any of the boys at school are bothering me. It's sweet.

Hey, what's that? Whoa, I think you might have... ZITS!

GASP!

Panel 3: Zits! That means I'll be a teenager soon!

Panel 4: Me and my friends are always playing at being teenagers. Teenagers are older than us. They go to the big school.

OH YEAH, THEY'RE JUST LIKE THE ONES MY SISTERS HAVE!

Cool, huh?

← *Cassandra and Eugénie*

Panel 5: When we play at being teenagers, we go out at night to a place without parents and we do whatever we want, like dancing (the waltz, etc.) and romancing.

You're so beautiful

Truly sublime

Panel 6: We only play with other girls. The boys in my school are total bastards (sorry about the swear word, but it's true). For example, at break time on the day I got my zits, we were playing and this is what happened.

Hey geeks! So do you touch each other's tits?

?

Panel 7: The boy who said that is called Abdou. He's in Year 6. He used to be nice but recently he's been horrible – and all because he wears a sleeveless leather jacket.

MIND YOUR OWN BUSINESS! GO AWAY!

You should tie your hair back, buy some clothes!

Make an effort! Wear leggings so we can see your arse! Ha ha!

All the boys dress like him

Panel 8: Abdou keeps bothering me. He's always saying stuff about love and dicks and I don't care about any of that.

Can I dance with you? It's better with a boy than with a girl...

Dancing real close...

Ha ha

Panel 9: MIIIISSSS THEY'RE HARASSING US! MIIISSS!

Panel 10: SHUT YOUR MOUTH, IDIOT! WITH YOUR TWO NIPS ON YOUR FOREHEAD!

I'M DOING YOU A FAVOUR!

Panel 11:

Panel 12: How was school today?

Panel 13:

Nips are what women have at the ends of their breasts, if you didn't know.

(Based on a true story told by Esther, who is 10 years old)

Riad Sattouf

The Hundred Years War

I don't like school. All the things we learn are boring.

This is me with my new hairstyle (it's better, right?)

We have the ugliest teacher in France

At the moment, for example, we're doing the Hundred Years War. It was a war (this thing where everybody hates each other and they fight) between the English and the French that lasted a hundred years.

People back then were really ugly

It's really annoying. I don't see the point of learning about stuff that happened so long ago.

Joan of Arc was 17 when she heard the voices of saints telling her to liberate France...

Take Joan of Arc, for example. She was a woman with a terrible haircut and she heard voices telling her to kill the English, so she did.

JOAN! GO KILL THE ENGLISH PLEASE!

Um... okay.

Completely crazy

Then she commanded an army. They were all men and they all obeyed her! Boys obeying a girl? Yeah, like THAT's believable.

ATTACK!

Go on!

We must obey! Her hair's so cool...

And after that, I don't really understand all this, but Joan had to help the dolphin Charles to become king. But that can't be right, can it? Dolphins live in the sea! Anyway...

Come on, we're off to Reims!

EEK EEK EEK

Joan of Arc won all the fights and killed the English, just like the voices told her, and she became the most popular girl in France despite her haircut.

GASP it's Joan of Arc! I wish I was her friend...

But after that, things went wrong and she was burned alive while people laughed their heads off! I mean, I may not like her, but that's a bit harsh.

Apparently, the people who did that later apologized.

Sorry I laughed, I was just nervous

... and that's why Joan of Arc is known as "the mother of the French nation"

Then Kalila asked a really interesting question.

Yes, Kalila?

Miss, there's something weird about the Hundred Years War in our history book, because it never talks about the Rebeus or the Renois... Did they do it on purpose not to mention them? Because there must have been some in the army and the cities and all that...

So maybe they did all the fighting really and Joan of Arc was a racist and she said "Yeah, we're not gonna mention them, let's just say it was us..."

Thank you, Kalila... I... Let's come back to that later...

And that's why I don't like school. We never talk about the really interesting stuff.

(Based on a true story told by Esther, who is 10 years old)

24

The Future

This is me at the moment.

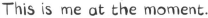

My parents hate the world of today. They don't want me to have a mobile phone before I go to secondary school...

... but they let me take singing and dancing classes instead

Tonight I can't sleep insomnia going crazy I can't be what I flee

Right now, we're working on this old song called "Assassymphonie" from "Mozart l'Opera Rock"

I'm really gifted! The teacher said that, not me

How do I see myself in four years? Well, I think I'll be a teenager, but not a bad one.

I'll have a hat and a phone, finally (but not an iPhone – my dad said "If you want an iPhone, get a job and pay for it yourself")

Curly hair, maybe (to see what it's like)

I'll wear "hip-hop" tops...

... and "feminine" skirts and shoes to balance it out

My friends will have zits and they'll be fat and ugly but I'll like them anyway

When I'm 18, I'll have finished school (can't wait!) and I'll try to make it as a singer.

On my road, yeah, there were moves, yeah, movie adventures, a life of roots, on my road, yeah, got no more worries...

I'll cover "Sur Ma Route" by Black M

I'll finally be blonde

Wow
Brilliant
1 2

Best thing I've ever heard
3 4

I'll wear baggy clothes so people will judge me purely on my voice

At 22, I'll probably be, you know, a massive star, performing all over the world.

L'amour à mort amore

I wrote those words

I'll look super-hot because that's what sells

After that, about 25, I'll have a boyfriend who's an actor, a dancer or a singer. And we'll be soulmates.

I'll be so famous that I'll have to wear disguises to go out

He'll have a cool dude hat

A goatee

A sleeveless leather jacket

We'll have four children (yes, I WANT four children – girls, if possible). I'll buy them each an iPhone when they're born so they'll have a better childhood than their mum.

I'll be happy

(Based on a true story told by Esther, who is 10 years old)

Riad Sattouf

Pretty Ill

We're a really happy family. We don't have any problems, to be honest.

I was pretty ill this week, and that made me happy.

I love it when I get ill because everybody looks after me. Well, my dad mostly.

The doctor came and he said what it was...

I also like being ill because I don't have to go to school. And this year, for the first time, I stayed at home alone. I could watch episodes of "Violetta" all day long.

It's an amazing show about the adventures of Violetta, this girl who becomes a singer like her dead mother.

"Violetta" is so exciting. It's about life and betrayal (and they all have iPhones too).

But the funniest thing about being ill is my brother.

It's always the same. He repeats the same stuff endlessly and thinks he's so clever...

Esther, can I ask you a favour? If you die, please come back and haunt our house! I really want to see something paranormal for once in my life.

I do it every time and I swear he doesn't even realize.

(Based on a true story told by Esther, who is 10 years old)

Riad Sattouf

26

The Killer Nutmeg Game

The person who makes me laugh most in the world is my dad.

I like laughing. It helps me deal with life at my private school.

When I finish Year 6, I'm supposed to go to the same free school as my brother. There aren't any private secondary schools around here.

So yeah, I'm supposed to go to the same school as him when I'm older.

My brother thinks he can scare me with his stories about the free school.

"It's this game that everybody plays, even girls... First, people stare each other out in the playground..."

"They get together and wait till there are no monitors around. Then they go upstairs and stand in a circle. They put a tube of glue on the ground and open their legs."

"Then they take it in turns to try to kick the tube of glue between the legs of another player. You have to close your legs really quickly."

"Whoever gets the tube of glue between his legs... has to let the others beat him up until he passes out."

I wasn't scared by this at all. In fact, I challenged Antoine to play the killer nutmeg game with me.

Sorry, but life doesn't scare me one bit.

(Based on a true story told by Esther, who is 10 years old)

Riad Sattouf

Youpaurne

I'm a pretty understanding person, but I'll never understand boys.

This is me thinking about my dad as I arrive at school

A Year 2 kid (who cares)

Today, for example, I was in the playground with Eugenie and Cassandra and we were talking about "Violetta" (only the best TV show in the world)...

He betrayed Violetta's trust

That's really bad, yo

... and then we saw the teacher running up to three boys: Louis (my ex-husband), Maxime (the best-looking boy in school) and Abdou (who's sometimes nice).

Hey! No mobile phones at school!

Haha fuck

WHASSUP WE'RE JUST TRYING TO GET ON YOUPORN!

Hee hee

PFHA HA HA HA

The teacher made this really weird face, like it was the most terrible thing ever.

Hngn I... you...

Then she took them to the headmaster and he called their parents to come and fetch them!

What's YOUPAURNE?

Dunno, it must be a game...

Miss, what's YOUPAURNE?

DON'T START, ESTHER!

YOUPAURNE – YOUPAURNE – YOUPAURNE... YOUPAURNE? YOUPAURNE... YOUPAURNE... YOUPAURNE – YOUPAURNE – YOUPAURNE!

Oh, by the way, does anyone know what YOUPAURNE is?

(Based on a true story told by Esther, who is 10 years old)

Riad Sattouf

YouPorn

Yesterday, Abdou, Louis and Maxime were punished because they went on "Youpaurne" at school.

This is my dad taking me to school

Me

I asked my parents what it was but they said they didn't know.

I love him SO much

My dad knows what it is, but he doesn't want to tell me! He can't hide anything from me – I'm his daughter. I felt sure they were talking about that with the teacher and some other parents.

?

I saw Eugenie (FYI: she has an iPhone 6 and I don't have a phone at all)

Esther, I have to tell you a secret!

I went on YouPorn on my phone yesterday, yo

It's this site full of videos of people making babies!

Eugenie saw a video of a girl who was being hit by the boy while they were making the baby! Too weird!

It was the most horrible thing I've ever seen!

I know what making babies is. It's when a man and a girl rub their... well, you get the idea.

OHH OHH OHH OHH OHH

Our neighbours are always making babies, but they don't have any children

Abdou, Maxime and Louis were told off by the headmaster and their parents were summoned to the school. But they're all very rich, so they don't care.

Hi Esther... We're going on YouPorn... You know what that is?

Oh yeah, "Youpaurne", that's good... go ahead... if you want to...

"OH YEAH, YOUPORN, THAT'S GOOD"?!? YOU KNOW IT!!!

YOU GO ON IT!!!

HA!

MMMMM ♥ Estherrrr!

♥ MMMMM ♥ that's hot

Afterwards, everybody said "Apparently, Esther goes on 'Youpaurne' too."

(Based on a true story told by Esther, who is 10 years old)

Riad Sattouf

The Rabbit

I adore my family.

My mum
My dad (who I love)
My brother Antoine (an idiot, obviously)
← Me

My favourite moment in life is when I go to bed. I close my eyes, think about nice food, and fall asleep in five seconds flat.

Me eating Oreos that fall from the sky

Almost every night, I have the same dream

I'm walking in the mountains with my parents.

Me in a princess dress

Just then, a rabbit arrives.

Your highness! I'm being chased by a hunter! Help me hide, please!

?

I hide it under my dress and then the hunter arrives.

God be praised!

Hello, your highness... You didn't happen to see a rabbit come this way, did you?

He looks like my dad but it's not him

No, no!

Are you sure?

Yes, yes!

A very small rabbit...

I have a feeling you're hiding something from me...

Me? Absolutely not

In the end he goes away and the little rabbit is saved!

Thank you, your highness! I owe you my life!

You're welcome, little rabbit! Be happy!

I used to love this dream...

... but last week, the rabbit did something else.

And to thank you, here's an iPhone 6!

It was amazing! I could go on the internet and everything!

Violetta

Then I woke up and I remembered that my dad didn't want me to have a phone until I went to secondary school. Life is a nightmare.

(Based on a true story told by Esther, who is 10 years old)

Riad Sattouf

The Film

This is me in my dad's arms.

Sometimes he carries me when I'm feeling tired ←

I'm allowed to watch films, especially Disney films.

♪ "Let it go, let it goooo" ♪

I know them all so well that I watch them upside down →

The other day my parents weren't home and my brother decided to watch a film called "Taken".

Can I watch it with you?

NAH it's not for children, it's too violent

I begged him and finally he let me.

I'll show it to you, but don't tell Dad! This is a real film, yo!

I PROMISE!

IT WAS THE BEST FILM I'D EVER SEEN.

You don't know it? It's the story of an American teenager who wants to go on holiday in Paris with a friend. But her dad's against it — he's afraid to let her leave (obviously, because he's her dad).

Call me as soon as you get there!

Of course! Bye!

Paris here we come!

They're about to get on the plane →

No sooner do they get to Paris than they're kidnapped by boys! But the girl just has time to call her dad.

Don't move, bitch

DAAAAD HELP!

When he finds out, the dad goes straight to Paris.

He's really angry because he used to be a policeman or something ←

Everybody in this film has a phone ←

And then he kills EVERYBODY so he can find his daughter. It's really scary but really nice too.

WHERE'S MY DAUGHTER?

Pleeease don't tell my parents

It's a film about boys and how they're all idiots.

WHERE'S MY DAUGHTER?

Kzzz

Kzzz

KZZZZZ

Anyway, at the end, the dad saves his daughter and it's wonderful.

My love

My baby

DAAAAD I LOVE YOU!

Calm down, we just went shopping

CASTORAM

We have to appreciate people while they're here because we never know what might happen to us in the future.

(Based on a true story told by Esther, who is 10 years old)

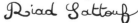

31

Cassandra

This time, I have a very sad story to tell you. I've already told you about my lovely friend Cassandra. She lives with her mum in a high-rise outside town. Every day, Cassandra has to ride fifteen stations on the metro just to come to school. She's really really poor: she always wears the same clothes because her mum uses all her money to pay for school. And worst of all, Cassandra's dad abandoned her when she was one year old. He went back to live in Martinique because he couldn't stand the cold weather in Paris. Cassandra always talks about him when it's sunny here.

She walked through the playground like that, and apart from us, nobody looked at her. We didn't know that Cassandra's mum had come to fetch her from school because her dad... well, he died in Martinique. When she found out, Cassandra said "Can I go to the toilet?" So she went and, when she didn't come back out, her mum and the headmaster went to see what was happening. And, well, Cassandra... she'd tried to take her own life by putting her head in the toilet and flushing it. That was a week ago and she still hasn't come back to school.

(Based on a true story told by Esther, who is 10 years old)

Riad Sattouf

The Other Child

This is us having a family picnic.

We're in the Bois de Boulogne

So, there's something that... I didn't want to talk about it before but now I feel like I can, so I'm just going to say it.

Esther, would you like some grated carrots?

I told you a million times I hate them, don't you ever listen to me?

?

My mum is pregnant.

HEY, DON'T YOU DARE TALK TO ME LIKE THAT!

Be polite, sweetheart

Haha

Whoa, whassup!

Esther the OG

I didn't want to talk about it before because "she" didn't really exist, but now my mum's belly is starting to get big (bigger than normal, I mean).

I say "she" because I'm sure it will be a girl. Us girls have special powers for sensing that kind of thing.

Women are sensitive to the rhythms of the universe

We are receivers of information

I read that in a horoscope or something

In my imagination, my sister is nothing like me. She has curly red hair (not blonde – there are no blondes in our family).

She has thick hair

Small eyes

Round nose

Fat cheeks

Gap teeth

"Tomboy" type

Big feet

If it was a boy... well, that would be okay too...

Esther, can you tell me if my feet stink?

FLUB!

He'd be like my brother but smaller

HA HA HA HA!

HEE HEE HEE HEE HEE HEE

But a girl would be better.

This is my "flamenco" dress. It's my favourite.

WHOA!

IT'S BEAUTIFUL

I would be her role model. I'd teach her how to get popular at school...

You'll need a new hairstyle. But with hair like yours...

Never mind, my love, you'll just have to be "the funny one"

MWAH

And how is Daddy's sweet little baby?

Gni!

Actually I don't understand why my parents are having another child. But, I mean, it's okay. I'm fine with it.

(Based on a true story told by Esther, who is 10 years old)

Riad Sattouf

The Gypsy

I'm a fan of Kendji Girac.

If you're old, you probably don't know Kendji Girac. He's THE favourite singer of all girls.

He's a "gypsy". I know what that is now. It's people who are always playing the guitar and who don't really have a house.

You see him running along train tracks. It's really good.

Kendji Girac: 1 – he's a good singer. 2 – he's very good-looking. 3 – he's "sensual".

"Sensual" means he would rather move and dance than talk. This is an excerpt from his video "Conmigo" (I don't know what that means, I think it's Latin or something).

Then he sees some enemies.

And now he's feeling love for the girl who's with the enemies.

He looks at her, and what flows between them without talking... that's it, "sensual".

She surrenders to him.

Anyway, if he doesn't know where to go next on his journey, he can always sleep here (just kidding).

(Based on a true story told by Esther, who is 10 years old)

Riad Sattouf

The Past

I can hardly remember anything from when I was very young. But I do remember a little bit. I remember being in my pram with my dad. But in the memories of my mother, it's like she's all hair and no face.

Another time, I remember I was at the pool and my brother was annoying me, then Dad yelled at him and everybody was staring.

I remember a cartoon about Rapunzel called "Tangled Ever After". They were at the church and Rapunzel was about to marry Flynn. But Maximus (the horse) lost the wedding rings and didn't find them until the last second... That's my first film memory.

Oh, and I also remember one time we were on holiday in Bain-de-Bretagne and it was night-time. Me and my dad were in the garden and he'd just got the first iPhone. That was the first time I ever saw one.

(Based on a true story told by Esther, who is 10 years old)

Riad Sattouf

Gunfire

Last Sunday I heard gunfire on the street! So I looked out the window.

This is me, in "what's going on?" mode

It was a boy throwing bangers

BANG! BANG!

His parents yelled at him in a foreign language. Everybody was watching from their window. They were a really weird family.

The dad could hardly walk

He'd been drinking, I think

BANG! BANG!

After a while, the dad sat down on the pavement and the mum shouted something and ran off.

BANG!

That was the only time the boy stopped throwing bangers. He went to see his dad and tried to help him up.

So the dad waved his hand like "get away from me" and the boy looked at me and I looked at him and I smiled and waved to be nice.

BANG!

THAT WAS A REALLY NASTY THING TO DO, DON'T YOU THINK?

(Based on a true story told by Esther, who is 10 years old)

Riad Sattouf

36

Sensitivity

Friday was the last day of school before the Easter holidays.

This is me sitting on my dad's back while he does press-ups →

Yeah, my dad is super-strong

And on that Friday, Mitchell — one of the most horrible boys at my school — did another weird thing.

This is him with his shorts and socks (so ugly) →

Nobody ever plays with him at break time, so he climbs onto a sort of bench near the wall and watches the street.

Waiting for break to end ↗

So anyway on Friday he suddenly started screaming like a lunatic.

AARRGH! AARRGH!

He sounded like a girl ↑

Everybody went to see what his problem was.

HEEEELP! HEEEELP!

AARRGH!

He'd seen a pigeon get squished by a car just outside the school.

AAAARRRGH!

It was DIS-GUS-TING!

Mitchell started crying and calling for the teacher and stuff...

MISS! WE HAVE TO HELP HIM! HE'S HUUUURRRRT!

...and so everybody started laughing and making fun of him to make him cry even more...

YEAH HE'S SOOOO HURT, HE'S TORN TO FUCKING PIECES! QUEER!

HAHA HAHAHA HA HA HAHA

VORTEX

← Maxime's impersonation was so funny

...and we laughed and laughed.

HA HA MITCHELL HA HA

Sorry if you're shocked, but us kids... if a pigeon dies, we laugh. That's just how it is.

Come on, it's over now... He's gone to pigeon heaven...

HA HA

Aheu! Aheu! Aheuuu!

Our super-ugly teacher

And no, I'm not "heartless". For example, sometimes I imagine my dad dying...

Miss, something terrible has happened...

...your father is dead.

...and I immediately start crying. That's <u>sensitivity</u>.

He was sliced in half by a horse-drawn carriage.

Daddy...

(Based on a true story told by Esther, who is 10 years old)

Riad Sattouf

37

The Gym

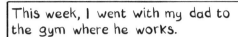
This week, I went with my dad to the gym where he works.

This is me and him in the special changing room for employees

We're getting dressed in sports clothes

You need to wear trainers that haven't been in the street

My dad is a really nice man. Honestly, even if he wasn't my dad, I'd still love him.

Hi Miguel, how are you? This is Esther, my princess

Hey Manu! How's it going?

He's a new teacher

Pleased to meet you, miss! What a beautiful girl — I bet she ends up a model.

Ha ha... she's got to finish school first

Everybody knows him. He's very popular. The customers all want him to themselves.

YO MANU!

All right, lads?

Could I have a word later?

But he treats everybody the same. He helps the super-sporty types...

Bend, Florence, down and then up again

UNGH

... and he helps people who go to the gym for the first time.

First, set a goal. What's your goal?

Um, to get muscly

But not too muscly

Okay, lads, the first thing you have to do is eat better to get rid of those bellies.

He makes them work their abs.

Aren't we hmmpf going to use the machines?

Until you get rid of that belly, the machines won't do you any good. Do another set of 15...

My dad is honest and sincere. There's a photo of him on a pillar in the gym.

He's just standing like that, between two walls in the corridor

He looks perfectly calm. Everybody can see that photo, and it shows them all that he's the strongest.

It brings tears to my eyes just looking at it

He's my dad and my role model. One day, I'll be like him.

For now, I can do this in my bathroom

(Based on a true story told by Esther, who is 10 years old)

Riad Sattouf

38

Little Bastard

I'm really sporty.

This is me doing the splits in our living room

I'm also very bendy

My dad loves sport (hardly surprising: he works in a gym), so we watch wrestling with him on TV.

My dad's really pleased when Antoine says that

Dad, I bet you could have been a professional wrestler

HA HA

Oh my God, he's challenging John Cena

Wrestling is men with big muscles fighting to see who's the strongest.

They always stare at each other angrily and say nasty things

They get into some really weird positions that hurt a lot. They're called "power moves".

YAHH!

COME ON SMASH HIM SMASH HIS FACE COME OOOOON! CRUSH HIM DAMN IT!

You dared to provoke me. You're going to regret it

My brother gets so excited when he watches wrestling and my dad thinks it's hilarious. He doesn't even tell Antoine off for swearing!

SMASH HIS STUPID BLOODY FACE THE BASTARD!

HAHA you know wrestling is all fake, right?

Afterwards, he usually wants to do the positions with me in our bedroom.

Little bastard loses!

Kh!

He calls me "little bastard" because one of the wrestlers on TV is a dwarf and that's his name.

Don't move, little bastard, or I'll do a "high-angle senton bomb"! You might die if you move!

He's getting ready, oh my God, he's climbed onto the top rope, he's going to destroy the little bastard, he's going to smash her!

WOAAAAAAAAH

KRK

It really made this noise

He tried to avoid me at the last second, so he fell onto his knees and dislocated his menixus (that's what it's called).

But your knee braces make you look like a real wrestler!

He chose to hurt himself rather than me — that was nice of him!

And here's the Undertaker oh my God he's going to

(Based on a true story told by Esther, who is 10 years old)

Riad Sattouf

The Orphanage

The only times in life when I'm ever bored are in school. It's pretty sad.

This is me in class

This week, I got 5 out of 20 in maths. Let's talk about something else...

My friend Cassandra came back to school. Her dad, who'd abandoned her when she was young, died in Martinique and she wanted to kill herself...

She was away a long time. We were happy to see her again. It's funny: the first game she wanted to play was the orphanage game!

C'mooon let's play it!

?

Seriously, yo?

The orphanage is a game we used to play in Year 4 (but we don't play it much any more). We're orphans and we go to an orphanage with a very strict headmistress.

You will obey because you have no family!

YES MIIIISSS!

Violet's good at being the headmistress

We have to follow all the rules and be very submissive.

Here you go, girls, you can eat the leftover dog food.

THANK YOU, MISS

You're too kind

Mmm!

But at night in the dormitory, one of us finds a hole in the wall.

Cassandra, where are you going?

I'm going to run away and hide in the forest!

Come back! That's not allowed! They'll whip you!

She goes to live "a natural life" in the forest.

Oh, the trees are full of fruit and if I get thirsty, I can drink river water...

Go back to sleep

I don't need anything. The forest will feed me!

This means a life of freedom, with no rules

She comes back at dawn and tries to convince the other orphans to go with her. So that's the game.

Run away with me! We can live freely, in nature!

No, we like the orphanage

It's too good for us!

When we played it before, none of the orphans wanted to leave. We all liked being good, obedient girls.

Go back to bed, the headmistress is coming!

What's going on?

Quick!

Come with me! I found a Samsung Galaxy Edge near the stream!

What?

Really cool phone

Her mum gave it to her to make her feel better after her dad died.

Everybody left the orphanage and we went to live "the natural life" in the bathroom with Cassandra.

Go ahead, I'll be the lookout...

GASP!

Whoa!

(Based on a true story told by Esther, who is 10 years old)

Riad Sattouf

40

Bad Girls

Abdou is a Year 6 boy who is sometimes nice and sometimes not (we don't know what's going on in his head). He's always talking about sex and stuff, he's obsessed, so anyway he was with his girlfriend and they were snogging in the toilets and then the other day they had a row and this is what he said.

GET AWAY FROM ME, YOU DIRTY HO!

We were really shocked Cassandra

Me   Eugenie

Apparently Claire had cheated on Abdou with a boy from her after-school club

Abdou was really angry

Aaaah, he called Claire a "DIR-TEE-HO"! That's bad, isn't it?

OMG

Did you see that?

Violet

I thought "dirty ho" was a bad way of saying "stupid idiot".

Nah, it's not that! My sister told me!

A "ho" is a girl who's so obsessed that she goes with lots of boys in exchange for presents or sometimes even money...

REALLY?

They're bad girls. Apparently only girls can be "hos". That's because we're basically pure, not like boys.

Waaaaah!

It'll be okay

See, girls are better than boys, because boys are obsessed. If a girl is obsessed, then she's just like a boy. There's nothing worse than that. So a ho is basically a boy.

I think that clears that up.

(Based on a true story told by Esther, who is 10 years old)

Riad Sattouf

Smells

I'm going to tell you about smells I like and smells I don't like.

I don't like the smell of perfume. My mum wears it sometimes (Nina Richy is the brand).

I like the smell when I'm in my dad's arms. He smells of sweat, even when he wears Mennen (a brand of perfume for men).

I don't like the smell of my brother in the bathroom.

I like the smell of the metro just in front of the tunnel.

I don't like the smell of alcohol.

I like the smell in the garage at my granny's house (we'll be going there soon).

I don't like the smell of cheese (unless it's melted).

But I love the smell of Four Cheese pizza from Pizza Pino.

I don't like the smell of steamed vegetables.

But the smell I love the best is the one that comes out of a brand-new iPhone box (I won't get one of my own until I go to secondary school).

(Based on a true story told by Esther, who is 10 years old)

Riad Sattouf

The Clown of Death

Just like every summer, we go to my granny's house in Bain-de-Bretagne at the start of the holidays.

This is me and my granny watching TV (there's no sound because she listens on headphones)

There's not much to do there, but at least I get to see my friend Eugenie 2.

She's put on so much weight, I'm shocked

Hello sweetheart!

Hey bella!

Her parents have separated since the last time I saw her and now she lives with just her mum in Nantes (I think that's in the south of France).

Not only has she put on weight but her eyes go really wide when she talks now

It was crazy

She told me that her mum works in a bar every night...

...and I stay at home alone... To start with, I liked it but now I'm really scared because sometimes I can hear someone coughing...

And I don't know if it's the neighbour or the Clown of Death...

Huh?

What, you've never seen the CLOWN OF DEATH?

Eugenie told me that when you brush your teeth in front of the mirror and look into your own eyes...

...the Clown of Death appears behind you...

...but when you look at him, he vanishes

He always appears when Mum's at work and I'm all alone...

...like the Legless Mute ...Have you seen her?

The Legless Mute is a dead woman (which is why she's mute) who walks on two fleshy stumps and waits near your bed so she can stroke you with her long, soft, disgusting fingers.

She doesn't touch you unless you move, so you have to hold very still

...

Now I'm in "scared-to-death" mode.

(Based on a true story told by Esther, who is 10 years old)

Riad Sattouf

The Police

One of the things I hate most in the world is dogs. I'm really scared of them.

I really really prefer cats.

When we're in Brittany visiting Granny, we sometimes go to Saint-Malo. It's a town with a beach.

There are always dogs running around with no leash.

Every time, they belong to old people with yellow hair and plastic jackets.

And last time, this is what happened...

Then the old people told the police that my dad had beaten their dog. When really it was the dog that attacked me!

My dad explained that he'd been defending me, but the police didn't understand.

But he's on a leash, sir.

Yeah but he wasn't before...

At last they understood and went away. My dad told me that you always had to be polite to the police and explain things to them until they understood, even if they were a bit slow, because they could be dangerous.

My dad quoted a line from a dead writer (called Jean Coco or something) about dogs.

"I prefer cats to dogs because there are no police cats."

(Based on a true story told by Esther, who is 10 years old)

44

The Taste of the Sea

I eat everything. Except anything that comes out of the sea.

This is me swimming in the sea (I like swimming, sometimes)

I hate fish, prawns, oysters, lobsters...

Grilled sea bream.

MMM!

YUCK!!!

My dad

I don't mind breaded fish, as long as it's really yellow...

...and nice and square.

What I really don't like is when you have to eat the whole animal.

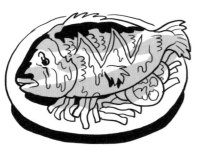

I see the poor thing suffering

I don't mind meat. You don't get this on your plate

But oysters are the worst.

You have to squeeze lemon juice on them to see if they're alive... They move, look!

My brother Antoine

Oh! It's so bright!

The light hurts their eyes

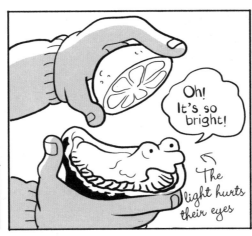

ARGH IT BURNS

And the sea is really dirty. Yesterday, we were at the beach and my brother needed to go to the toilet.

Just go in the sea. It's not a big deal.

Ahhhhh!

HAHA! Feel better?

The fish will be pleased.

Yeah ha ha

How can anyone eat a creature that feeds on Antoine's poo?

(Based on a true story told by Esther, who is 10 years old)

Riad Sattouf

The Dead Singer

At my granny's house, I discovered an unknown French singer with the most beautiful voice. His name was Daniel Balavoine. My grandmother had all his albums. He was a sensitive, misunderstood artist who lived a long time ago.

Here he is on this poster that Granny gave me. Okay, he's not very good-looking (a little chubby) but that's why I get so emotional about him. He hated himself and he wanted to be loved

Music was his world

DANIEL BALAVOINE

This song is called "Le Chanteur". It's about his dreams

And everywhere in the street
I want them to talk about me
I want naked girls
To throw themselves at me
To admire me and to kill me
To take my virginity
I want to be an idol
For the girls at my old school
Every night I want them
Breathless in their beds
To cheat on their husbands with me
Endlessly in their dreams

I can't stop crying when I listen to these lyrics

I don't understand why he's not more famous

One day in Africa, he got in a helicopter because another passenger was late and the helicopter crashed. It's horrible but he DIED, just like that. Without ever achieving his dreams. It's so unfair! I really hope I don't die before I achieve my dreams (make at least one album and perform at least one stadium concert).

(Based on a true story told by Esther, who is 10 years old)

Riad Sattouf

Lucio

After Brittany, I went to a summer camp, like I do every year.

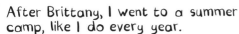

This is me telling my dad it's nice of him but he doesn't have to come with me all the way to the door of the train

The camp is a place where there are just kids and no parents and we can do activities.

TAKE CARE, DAD!

Eugenie came with me. It was her first time!

And this year, at the station, something wonderful happened...

We were waiting on the platform with loads of other campers

...a boy came over to speak to me.

Yo, you're gonna find out what **LUCIO** thinks of you later.

HUH? Who?

He left, and another boy appeared...

Hey skirt! **LUCIO** wants to talk to you. He wants to tell you something 'bout you and him.

...and then a girl took me by the hand...

LUCIO told me to come and get you.

...and led me over to this mysterious boy... who was only the best-looking boy I've ever seen!

Excellent cap

"Diamond" earring

Expensive American-style jacket

Yo, just wanted to tell you that you're the freshest girl in this train station

"Fresh" means really beautiful

Cool-dude hand movements

He was at least 12 years old!!!

Suddenly I felt overwhelmed...

You got a 6?

Um actually no but

He'd seen me from a distance

We didn't know each other!

HE KISSED ME ON **THE MOUTH!**

...then he caught his train and I caught mine. I gave him my dad's number so he could send me the selfie we took before we said goodbye.

Our affair lasted less than 45 minutes.

Our goodbye selfie

(Based on a true story told by Esther, who is 10 years old)

Riad Sattouf

Enzo

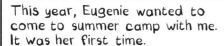

This year, Eugenie wanted to come to summer camp with me. It was her first time.

This is us trying to watch a Kendji video but the reception on the train was bad

I like going to summer camp because you meet new people. For example, this time I met Romane, a girl who loves to sing!

I smoke big joints and almost choke! Got two left I stuff 'em full and smoke!

♪♪

HAHA THAT'S FUNNY!

She's singing a track by Jul (he's a rapper) in "crazy" mode.

The boys here are not like the ones at my school. They all have footballer hair for a start.

They keep walking up and down the corridor like they have somewhere to go

I'll smash him

GO 'HEAD YO!

They talk with an accent like rappers and they only ever talk about fighting.

FUCK DAT DUDE WHATCHA WAITING FOR?

AN' HE SAID TO ME "YO, YOU LOOKIN' FOR TROUBLE?" FUCK HIS HO MAMA!

He's wearing a hoodie even though it's hot

Oh, and they're also really trashy and obsessed (even more than the boys at my school, I mean).

Excuse me, I wanted to ask you...

Do you think you're a good kisser?

Lick my tongue and I'll give you my opinion

LET ME GO!

HEY MOFO WHATCHA DOIN'? DON'T TOUCH HER, YO!

CHIIILLL

Don't worry, Enzo's just being a dick cos everybody calls him Pogba cos he looks like Pogba and he thinks he's as popular as Pogba but he ain't no Pogba..

YO

"Pogba" is a very rich footballer

When we got to the camp, they told us that we'd be put in rooms for two.

When you've found your roomie, go over there.

Wanna be with me?

YEAAH!

Eugenie didn't understand. She thought we would be in the same room together.

Listen, we see each other all year. We can take a break for two weeks, don't you think?

You know girls like me make boys like you cry You think you can handle me at first, and that's fiine...

♪ ♪ ♪

Brilliant impersonation of Vitaa singing "Game Over"

Romane is just great.

(Based on a true story told by Esther, who is 10 years old)

Riad Sattouf

48

Ormythology

The summer camp is in Arcachon (which is near Brittany, I think).

This is me and Romane, my cool new friend
Heyyy
The monitors

What's great about camp is that they have tons of different activities every day.

Who you thinking 'bout when I come in on the beeeeat?

She sings "Game Over" all day, it's so long, it's so cool

For example, we go out to look at birds. It's called ormythology.

Now tell me who puts the pressure on the beeeeat!

KWAK! KWAK!

Birds are creatures with wings and they fly (I think everybody knows that).

By the way, the monitor has a tattoo on her back and I keep wondering how far down it goes

We saw a sort of big white bird with a long straight neck that used to be a dinosaur (the guide told us that) but I can't remember its name.

Yeah, that's what I saw

Yes, it really did have a tail

And I swear you could see its teeth

Anybody know what it's called?

Birds have eyes on either side. They don't see ahead like we do. That means they look sideways as they go forwards.

Poor things

It's really difficult — I tried

We were interested but we didn't see much. It was mostly just seagulls.

Here's one

At one point, a small blue bird flew past really fast. But the guide was chatting with the monitor and he didn't see it.

HEY, IT'S A KINGFISHER! A FREAKING KINGFISHER, YO!

This is Enzo but everybody calls him Pogba

FLY EMIRATES

Whassup, man? Whaddja see?

A KINGFISHER! THERE WAS A KINGFISHER!

It's true, sir. We saw it too!

Finally the guide saw it too and everybody was happy because it's a really beautiful bird.

It looked at us

Super-cute

I really wish I could have one in my bedroom in Paris

It's weird that Enzo knows the names of birds and all that, don't you think? What a geek

Yeah, totally

(Based on a true story told by Esther, who is 10 years old)

Riad Sattouf

Rachida

I like summer camp. You meet cool new people.

This is me and Romane doing a dance routine in our bedroom

♪ She loved me with all her heart And all her soul She gave me all she had When I had nothing at all ♪

"Elle m'a aimé" by Kendji

Romane is my new friend. She's really great.

...and now...Esther... and Rachida...okay, you can take a shower now

NOT RACHIDA! CALL ME ROMANE!

In fact, Romane's real name is Rachida! WEIRD, huh?

Honestly, you don't look Arab at all

HEY, YOU SHOULDN'T SAY "ARAB" — THAT'S CISTRA, YO!

"Cistra" means "racist"

I'm a REBEUE. That's what you should say.

Romane also taught me that you shouldn't say "blacks" if you're talking about people who are, well, y'know, a colour.

You say "RENOIS".

I knew that, yo

You're white, and you're French. You don't say "Yeah, hi, I'm Esther the white girl". But you could say "Yeah, I'm French"

So anyway, Romane told me she was REBEUE but it got on her nerves because she hates her dad (who's Rebeu). She wants the monitor to tell her dad that she called herself Romane, to piss him off (sorry for the swear word).

Then she cried, poor thing

I bet he couldn't care less

There were lots of Renois and Rebeus on this summer camp because they come from poor neighbourhoods and the local government pays for them.

They're at free schools

It makes me feel bad

Anyway, we took a shower and Enzo came up and lifted Romane's towel so he could see her naked.

YAAAH! GASP!

I got really really annoyed.

PISS OFF RAPIST!

Hey, don't talk for me, yo! What if I wanted him to check out my arse?

But you

Whatever! Just don't do it again, 'kay?

Nobody decides for me!

I'm so sorry Esther I didn't mean to be rude to you but I reeeally love Enzo oh I love him so much...

sob

Romane is great, but she's kind of complicated.

(Based on a true story told by Esther, who is 10 years old)

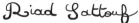

Dance Night

You have to pay for summer camp, even if most of the kids there are from free schools. This year, I met some really great people, for example my new best friend Romane (her real name's Rachida, but she wants everybody to call her Romane). On the last night, the monitors organized a dance and we were allowed to choose the music ourselves.

(Based on a true story told by Esther, who is 10 years old)

Riad Sattouf

Very Sad Days

Here's something I've noticed: sometimes in life you have happy days and sometimes you have very sad days.

This is me leaving summer camp with my new friend Romane

I got so upset when we said goodbye (even if we agreed that we'd see each other again)...

My dad

Well, it's nice to see that you're happy to be home!

Nobody came to fetch her. She went on the metro all alone

To make me feel better, my dad (who I love so much, and yes, I do tell him) bought me the three things I most love to eat (apart from Four Cheese pizza from Pizza Pino)!

Food is very important to me

You're the best, Dad!

First I had Zapetti ravioli. Heaven in a tin.

800g just for me!

Yum yum

I like it when my dad opens the tin. This delicious smell comes out – the smell of Italy.

SNFF

Pizza, ravioli... yeah, I love Italian food!

I like to eat three or four cold ravioli straight from the tin, before warming up the rest.

You can really smell the tomato when it's cold

And the sauce is thicker

You're looking happier already

For dessert, my dad bought me my favourite fruit: a giant yellow mango.

It weighed at least a kilo (all for me!)

What I like best is when I scrape the inside of the skin with my teeth. You get all these juicy yellow threads.

I save the stone for last

But best of all was the big bag of sour lime-flavoured Head Bangers (my favourite sweets in the world).

They're so sour that I wonder if they might be dangerous

They give me a shock every time.

KRAK

I wonder if anybody has thought of making super-sour mango ravioli (I don't know why I said that, I must be going crazy).

XZSCHK

My mum is at my grandmother's house and my brother's at camp, but I miss Romane more than either of them.

Is it life or the sweets that are making me cry? I don't know

(I finished the whole bag of Head Bangers in one night.)

(Based on a true story told by Esther, who is 10 years old)

52

Fly Minerate

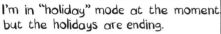

I'm in "holiday" mode at the moment but the holidays are ending.

This is me staring sadly through my window at the rain falling on Paris

There was a big problem this week, when my dad went to the train station to pick up Antoine (he'd been at summer camp).

YOU'RE A PAIN IN THE ARSE! YOU HEAR ME? I'M SICK OF YOU!

Hey, it's my body I can do what I want I don't give a crap what you...

I'd never seen my dad this annoyed before!

IN MY HOUSE YOU'D BETTER GIVE A CRAP, BOY!

He was in "fight" mode

My brother had got a footballer haircut during summer camp!

My dad had always told him not to get his hair cut like that. He said it was the devil's haircut

All boys love football and they've got "Fly Minerate" or something written on the shirt. I don't even know what that means

He had the same hairstyle and shirt as his hero Jeremy Menez (he's a footballer)

Before summer camp, he looked like this

He doesn't just look stupid, he really is

My dad called the summer camp and yelled at them that he wanted his money back.

I won't tell you everything that happened, but my dad smashed my brother's headphones against the wall to punish him.

He cried so much, I felt sorry for him

There was a mark on the wall

After that, he wore sunglasses and stayed up all night on his phone. Weird

I think I might wait till next week before I tell my dad that I want a new look too...

(Based on a true story told by Esther, who is 10 years old)

Riad Sattouf

Breasts

And now the holidays are over. Actually, I always enjoy going back to school. It's like a new start.

Cool, yo!

This is me with my new look

Think: hip, sporty, bendy

I changed a lot this summer (I've been through some stuff). I like the "dynamism" of my new outfit.

Cap on backwards because it's fun to bend the rules a bit

I'm in Year 6 now. I'm one of the big kids.

Here, Dad, I don't think I'll wear it after all

At the last minute, I just decided the cap was a bit too much

Everybody had a new look — it was funny!

HEY BABE!

Hee Hee

Cassandra had a new hairstyle!

I was so happy to see her again

So, anyway, I saw all my friends again, but I think it's over with Eugenie.

HI THERE!

!

She has a new look too

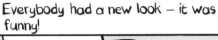

She said hello to Cassandra and totally blanked me

We didn't really hang out at the summer camp in July and we haven't been in touch since.

She's acting like she thinks she's a teenager already

Then we met our new teacher, who is just really weird.

I'm Mishuzh Rodriguezhhh mmm. Everybody in line pleazhe mmm

She's not actually a dwarf, she's just really short.

Ready, girlzh and boyzh mmm? Then letsh go mmm

Yep, she's the same height as me

Honestly, where does this school find its teachers? After ten minutes, I'd had it with her "mmms" at the end of every sentence.

Mrs Rodriguez

You can jusht call me mish mmm

They've mixed us all up, so I don't know many people in my class. Only Cassandra, Eugenie, Mitchell and two others.

Mitchell, the worst boy in the class, hasn't changed at all unfortunately

Eugenie sat at the front. She took off her jacket and turned to me. I saw pure hate in her eyes. I was really shocked.

She was in "enemy" mode

Oh, and another shock: SHE HAS BREASTS NOW

(Based on a true story told by Esther, who is 10 years old)

NEXT IN THE SERIES:

Riad Sattouf

ESTHER'S NOTEBOOKS

Tales from my eleven-year-old life

Pushkin Press

Pushkin Press
71–75 Shelton Street
London WC2H 9JQ

The graphic novel *Les cahiers d'Esther volume 1*
by Riad Sattouf was first published in French in 2016 by Allary Éditions.
© Allary Éditions and Riad Sattouf

English translation © Sam Taylor 2021

First published by Pushkin Press in 2021

These stories were pre-published in *L'Obs* between October 2014 and October 2015.

Thanks to Matthieu Croissandeau

INSTITUT
FRANÇAIS

This book is supported by the Institut français (Royaume-Uni) as part of the Burgess programme

1 3 5 7 9 8 6 4 2

ISBN 13: 978-1-78227-617-3

English version designed by Tetragon and Lucie Cohen

Printed and bound in Italy by Printer Trento SRL

www.pushkinpress.com